j623.82   Kerr, Daisy.
KER
          Ships.

$23.00

# ships

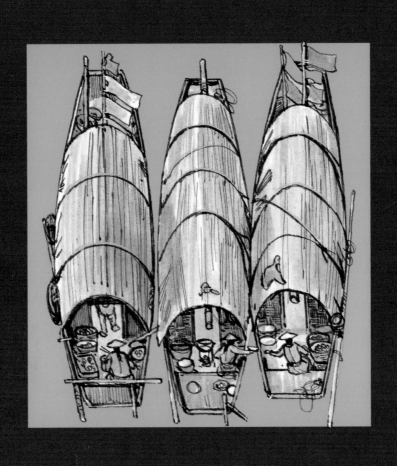

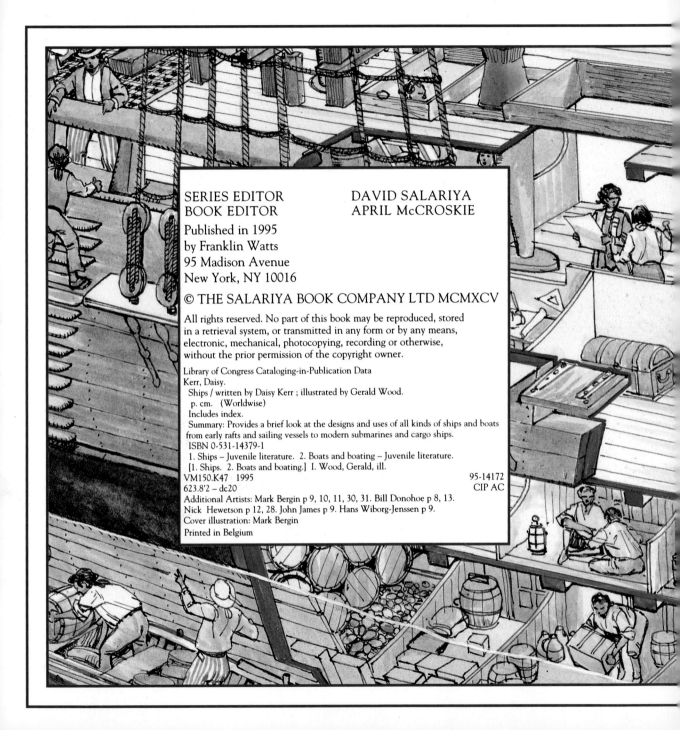

SERIES EDITOR    DAVID SALARIYA
BOOK EDITOR    APRIL McCROSKIE

Published in 1995
by Franklin Watts
95 Madison Avenue
New York, NY 10016

Library of Congress Cataloging-in-Publication Data
Kerr, Daisy.
  Ships / written by Daisy Kerr ; illustrated by Gerald Wood.
  p. cm.   (Worldwise)
  Includes index.
  Summary: Provides a brief look at the designs and uses of all kinds of ships and boats
from early rafts and sailing vessels to modern submarines and cargo ships.
  ISBN 0-531-14379-1
  1. Ships – Juvenile literature.  2. Boats and boating – Juvenile literature.
  [1. Ships.  2. Boats and boating.]  I. Wood, Gerald, ill.
VM150.K47  1995                95-14172
623.8'2 – dc20                   CIP AC
Additional Artists: Mark Bergin p 9, 10, 11, 30, 31. Bill Donohoe p 8, 13.
Nick Hewetson p 12, 28. John James p 9. Hans Wiborg-Jenssen p 9.
Cover illustration: Mark Bergin
Printed in Belgium

# worldwise
# ships

Written by
DAISY KERR
Illustrated by
GERALD WOOD

Series Created & Designed by
DAVID SALARIYA

# FRANKLIN WATTS
A Division of Grolier Publishing
New York • London • Hong Kong
Sydney • Danbury , Connecticut

# CONTENTS

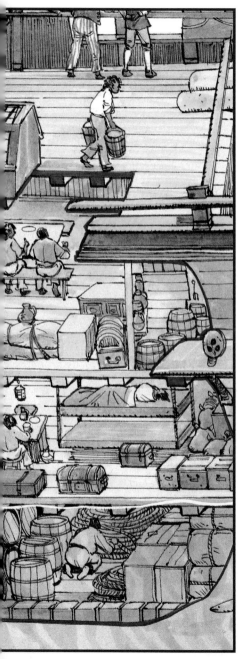

**Ships and boats** carry us safely over the water. They are built in many different shapes and sizes. Huge oil tankers carry loads of half a million tons. But on tiny jet skis, there is room for only one or two people aboard.

Long ago, the word "ship" meant a sailing craft with three masts. Today, large craft are called ships and smaller craft are called boats.

Ships and boats have been used for ferrying and fighting, as homes and for vacations, for adventuring and exploring – and just for fun. You can read about them in this book.

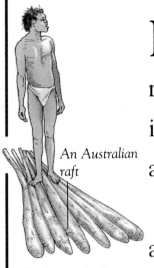

*An Australian raft*

# Discovering how to make boats meant that people could travel much farther in order to trade, go hunting, or to search for a better place to live.

The earliest boats were wooden logs or air-filled animal skins. Travelers sat on these as they floated downstream. Around 12,000 years ago, people learned how to hollow the center of a log to make a canoe. To do this they used flint axes, animal horns, and fire. They made paddles and sails also, so they could turn the boat in any direction.

**Rafts** made from bundles of logs tied together have been made for thousands of years.

*A boat from Vietnam*

**Boats** made from strips of bamboo are used to travel down wide rivers in Vietnam. They are pushed along with poles.

*Gufa*

**A gufa** is an Iraqi boat. It is made from reeds and coated with bitumen (a kind of tar) to make it waterproof.

*Floats of animal skin*

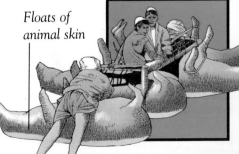

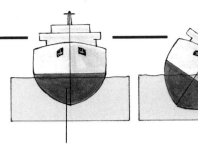

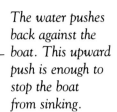

*The water pushes back against the boat. This upward push is enough to stop the boat from sinking.*

*A boat pushes aside the water it is floating in. Heavy boats push aside more water than light ones.*

**The ancient Egyptians** made boats out of the reeds that grew in shallow water close to the riverbank.
In Peru, fishermen still use reed boats.

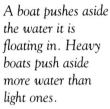

*Mast to hold the sail*

*Bow, or front, of boat*

*Oars to steer with*

*Egyptian cargo boat*

**Hydrofoils** are not boats, because they do not float. They travel on "foils" (like waterskis) that skim the water surface.

*Rubber "skirt" traps air*

**Hovercraft** are not boats because they hover above water. They float on a cushion of air produced by a fan.

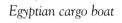

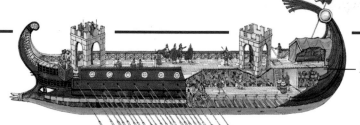
— *Roman galley*

**Roman galleys** were built to carry cargo or soldiers. They were heavy and difficult to steer. Warships had little castles on deck to protect soldiers.

# Rowing boats rely on muscle-power.

Before machines were invented, oars were the quickest way of propelling a boat. Paddles and poles were light and easy to use but oars produced much more power. Ships needed lots of rowers. Greek trieres (warships) were rowed by 170 men. Large Roman ships needed over 1,500 rowers if they wanted to travel fast.

*Painted eye keeps away bad luck*

*Punt*

*Gondola*

*Royal barge*

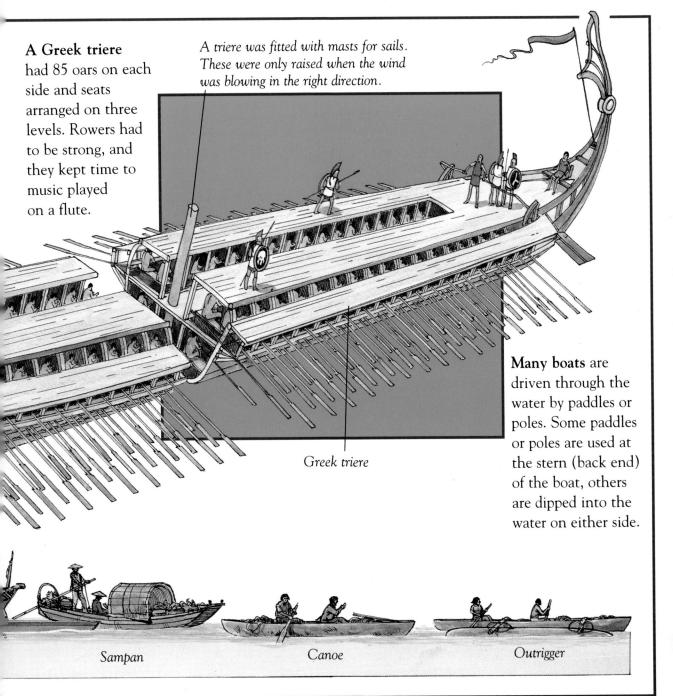

**A Greek triere** had 85 oars on each side and seats arranged on three levels. Rowers had to be strong, and they kept time to music played on a flute.

*A triere was fitted with masts for sails. These were only raised when the wind was blowing in the right direction.*

Greek triere

**Many boats** are driven through the water by paddles or poles. Some paddles or poles are used at the stern (back end) of the boat, others are dipped into the water on either side.

*Sampan*

*Canoe*

*Outrigger*

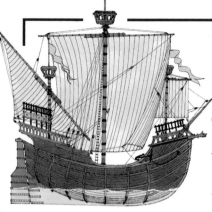

*Carrack (cargo ship)*

**Carracks** were built in Europe between 1350 and 1600. Their sails were on three tall masts.

*Wa'a kaula*

**A wa'a kaula** is a double canoe. Around 1400, Pacific Islanders used them to reach New Zealand.

Sails trap the wind and use it to drive a ship along. Big sails trap more wind. When the wind is blowing from the right direction, sailing ships can travel faster than rowing boats. If they want to sail against the wind, they have to steer a zigzag course. This is called tacking, and is very slow.

Sudden gusts of wind can capsize a ship (turn it upside down). Junks and modern sailing craft are designed with air pockets to help them stay afloat.

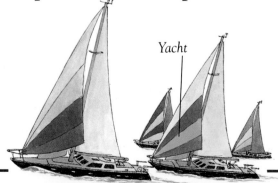

*Yacht*

**Yachts** are small sailing ships used for cruising, pleasure trips, and races. There is not much shelter aboard a yacht.

*Tea clipper*

Bamboo poles

Lugsail

**Tea clippers** were the fastest sailing ships. In the 1850s, they carried cargoes of tea and other valuable goods from India and China to Europe.

*A Chinese junk*

**Junks** have been around since 1200. They are steered by a rudder (like a paddle). Rudders can be raised or lowered for shallow or deep water.

**The sails** on junks are called lugsails. This means, "sails with four sides." They are made of canvas (heavy cloth) and bamboo poles called battens.

*The back end is painted red to scare away evil spirits.*

# European sailors

explored the oceans between 1450 and 1650. Christopher Columbus, from Italy, sailed across the Atlantic in 1492. He won fame as the first European to reach America. But Viking explorer, Leif Erikson, had sailed there almost 500 years before. Ferdinand Magellan's ship, from Spain, made the first voyage around the world. It took nearly three years, from 1519 to 1522. As you will see on pages 16 and 17, explorers bringing home treasure might be attacked by pirates.

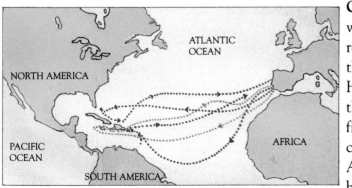

ATLANTIC OCEAN

NORTH AMERICA

PACIFIC OCEAN

AFRICA

SOUTH AMERICA

**Columbus** sailed west, hoping to reach Japan and the Spice Islands. He did not know that he would find an enormous continent – America – in his way.

*Niña*

**Columbus** and his crew made their voyage in three ships: the Pinta, the Niña, and the Santa Maria.

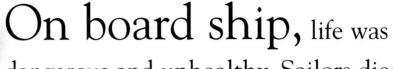

# On board ship, life was dangerous and unhealthy. Sailors died in battle, from fever carried by rats, or from bad food. Every day they had to work hard mending rigging, polishing cannon, and scrubbing decks. Some men had special tasks. They were sail-makers, doctors, and cooks. The whole crew had to fight if an enemy approached. Women could not be sailors – everyone believed they brought bad luck.

**A "man of war"** was a fighting ship. Ships like this were built in many European countries between 1600 and 1850. They needed a crew of 1,500 men to sail them.

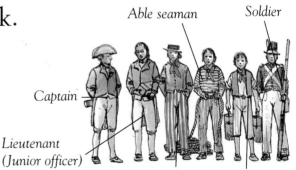

Captain

Lieutenant (Junior officer)

Able seaman

Soldier

Gunner    "Powder monkey"

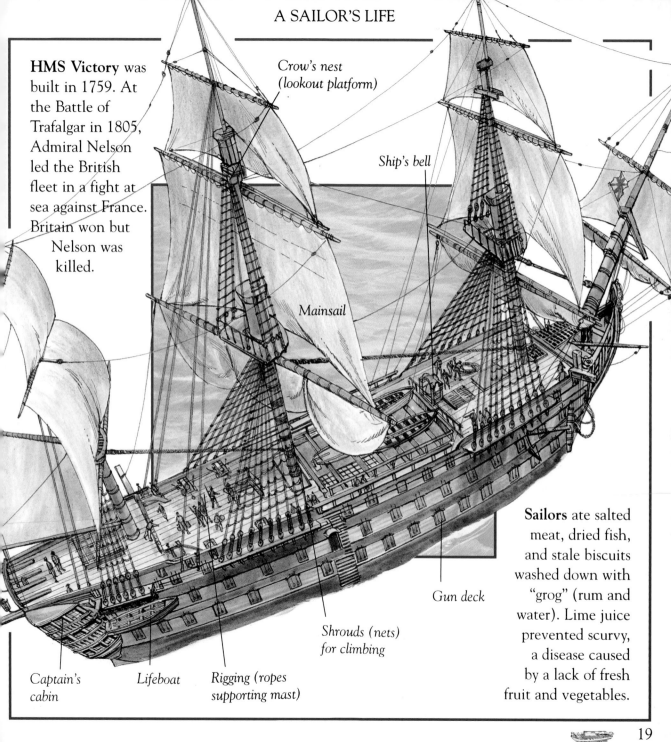

**HMS Victory** was built in 1759. At the Battle of Trafalgar in 1805, Admiral Nelson led the British fleet in a fight at sea against France. Britain won but Nelson was killed.

*Crow's nest (lookout platform)*

*Ship's bell*

*Mainsail*

**Sailors** ate salted meat, dried fish, and stale biscuits washed down with "grog" (rum and water). Lime juice prevented scurvy, a disease caused by a lack of fresh fruit and vegetables.

*Gun deck*

*Shrouds (nets) for climbing*

*Captain's cabin*

*Lifeboat*

*Rigging (ropes supporting mast)*

19

*This paddle steamer from around 1850, was built to travel along the Mississippi River.*

*Charlotte Dundas*

**The Charlotte Dundas** was the first successful steam-powered boat. It was launched in 1802.

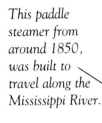

Cabin

Paddle wheel

Galley (kitchen)

Pilot house

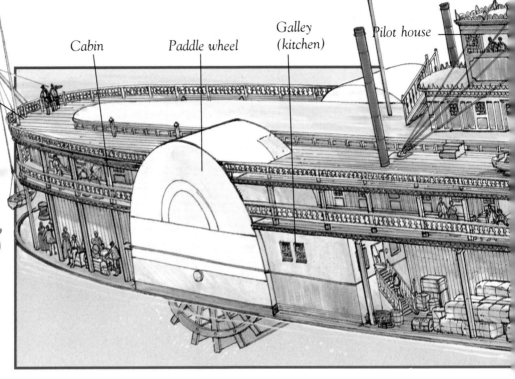

*Each paddle wheel had flat wooden blades. They were pushed into the water as the wheels turned around.*

# The steam engine was designed in 1769, by engineer James Watt. The power it produced could drive a boat. Steam engines caused a revolution in ship design. Now, steam-powered ships could sail long distances even if there was no wind.

Viewing balcony

Main deck

Paddle steamers were driven by huge steam-powered wheels. Later ships had steam-powered propellers placed at the stern. In 1845 it was proved that propellers worked better than wheels.

*The Great Eastern, 1858, was designed by Brunel, a British engineer. It was six times bigger than any other ship*

# In the past, all kinds of ferryboats, sailing ships, and steamers were used to take people across the sea. But special passenger ships to carry lots of people long distances in comfort were not built until 150 years ago.

*From around 1600 until 1865, ships crammed with black slaves from Africa sailed to white-owned sugar plantations in America and the Caribbean.*

*The Oriana is 900 ft (275 m) long and 98 ft (30 m) wide. It can carry 1,760 passengers and 760 crew on luxury cruises.*

Modern passenger ships, called "liners," are like floating hotels, with shops, movies, and swimming pools on board. The crew sails the ship and helps passengers enjoy themselves.

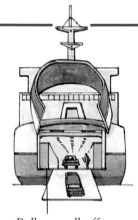

*Roll-on, roll-off ferries carry cars, trucks, and people. They have wide doors in the bow so that vehicles can be driven on board easily.*

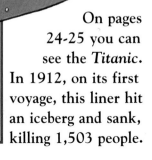

ORIANA

P&O

On pages 24-25 you can see the *Titanic*. In 1912, on its first voyage, this liner hit an iceberg and sank, killing 1,503 people.

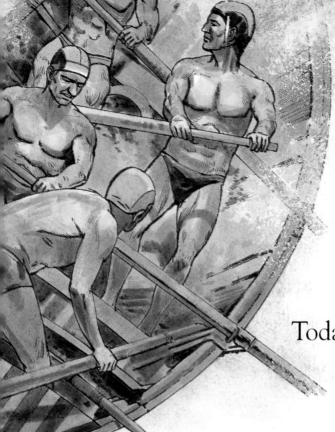

Sailors know the sea is a dangerous place, and there are rocks and sandbanks all around the coast. In the past, sailors with good eyesight were given jobs as lookouts. Today, ships have navigation aids that help them steer clear of dangers, even in the dark. But there are still some accidents at sea. These may be caused by engine failure or bad weather. Then sailors will send an "SOS" message, calling for help. They know that a lifeboat, with its brave crew of volunteers, will try to save them.

**In Australia,** some beaches have huge waves. Lifeguards keep watch, ready to row out in specially designed boats to save swimmers from drowning.

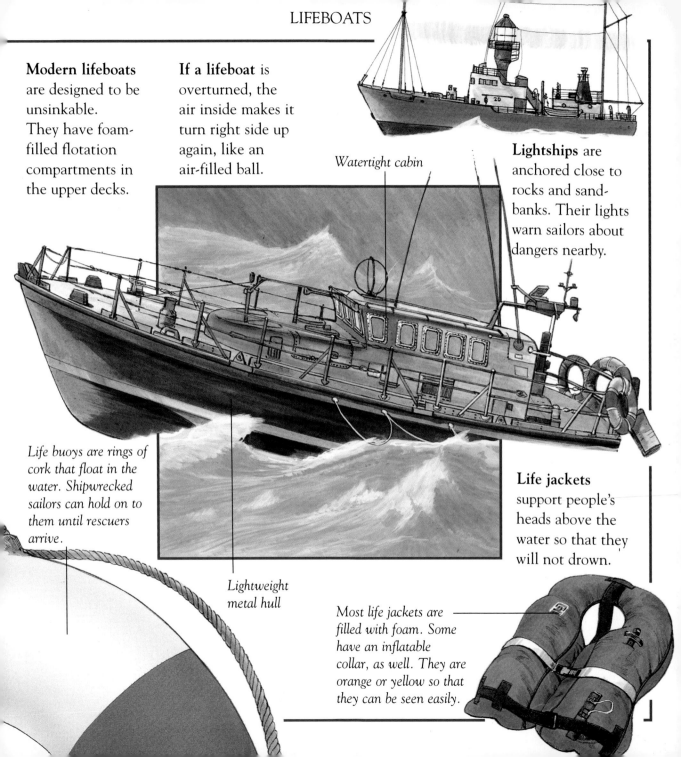

**Modern lifeboats** are designed to be unsinkable. They have foam-filled flotation compartments in the upper decks.

**If a lifeboat** is overturned, the air inside makes it turn right side up again, like an air-filled ball.

*Watertight cabin*

**Lightships** are anchored close to rocks and sand-banks. Their lights warn sailors about dangers nearby.

*Life buoys are rings of cork that float in the water. Shipwrecked sailors can hold on to them until rescuers arrive.*

*Lightweight metal hull*

**Life jackets** support people's heads above the water so that they will not drown.

*Most life jackets are filled with foam. Some have an inflatable collar, as well. They are orange or yellow so that they can be seen easily.*

*Dragon ship*

Ships have been used to fight in many different ways. Greek and Roman sailors sank enemy ships by ramming them under water. Around A.D. 800 Viking warriors used fast, sleek ships to make surprise raids. After 1500, sailors fired cannon to smash holes in enemy ships. By 1870, warships had bigger guns armed with exploding shells. Today, aircraft carriers act as mobile launching pads bringing missiles, helicopters, and planes close to enemy targets.

**Viking** warriors traveled in long "dragon ships." They hung their shields in rows along the side.

**Around** 1300, warships had "castles" at each end, where soldiers could shoot arrows.

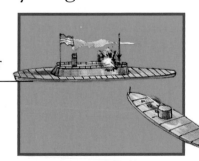

*Many ships of the American Civil War (1861-1865) were covered with iron plating to protect them from enemy gunfire.*

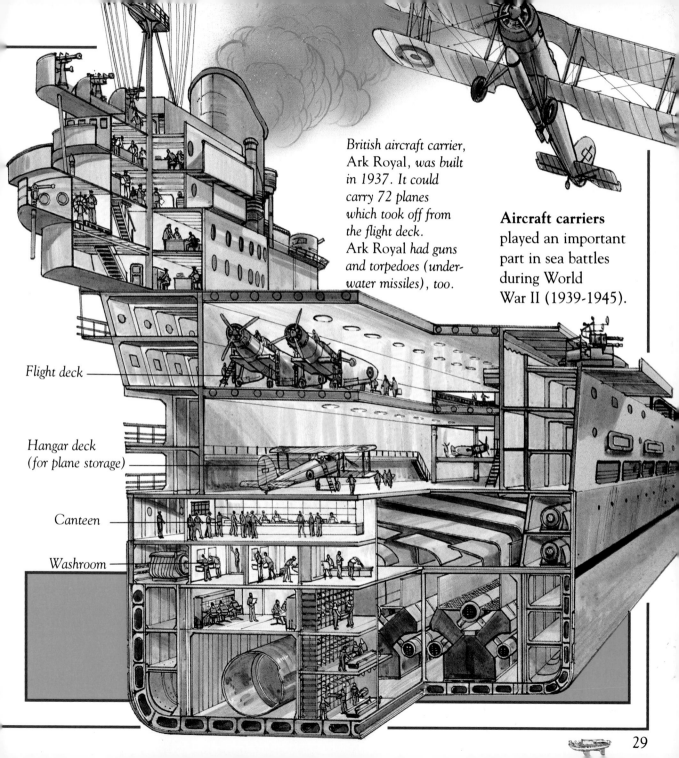

British aircraft carrier, Ark Royal, *was built in 1937. It could carry 72 planes which took off from the flight deck.* Ark Royal *had guns and torpedoes (underwater missiles), too.*

**Aircraft carriers** played an important part in sea battles during World War II (1939-1945).

Flight deck

Hangar deck (for plane storage)

Canteen

Washroom

**Modern submarines** are driven through the water by nuclear-powered propellers.

**Some David-class** metal-hulled submarines were driven by steam engines or hand-driven by sailors.

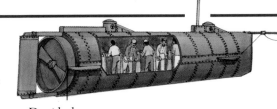

David-class submarine, 1860s

Nuclear missile

Rudder

Propeller

Engine room

Reactor room

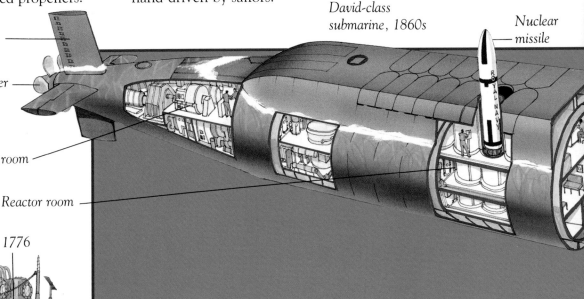

Turtle, 1776

**The wooden Turtle** submarine was the first underwater craft to be used in war. It could carry one person only.

# Submarines stay below the sea's surface to make surprise attacks on enemy ships. Mini robot submarines repair underwater pipelines and explore the deep-sea world. Some big submarines can stay underwater for two or three years.

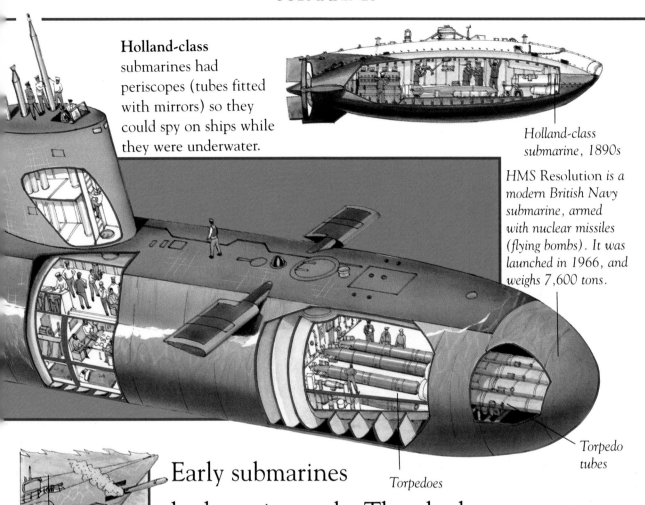

**Holland-class** submarines had periscopes (tubes fitted with mirrors) so they could spy on ships while they were underwater.

*Holland-class submarine, 1890s*

*HMS Resolution is a modern British Navy submarine, armed with nuclear missiles (flying bombs). It was launched in 1966, and weighs 7,600 tons.*

*Torpedo tubes*

*Torpedoes*

*U-Boat, 1939-1945*

**German submarines** (called U-Boats) sank hundreds of British ships during World War II.

Early submarines had no air supply. They had to return to the surface before the air inside ran out. Later submarines had breathing tubes, called snorkels. Today, most submarines can recycle the air they have on board.

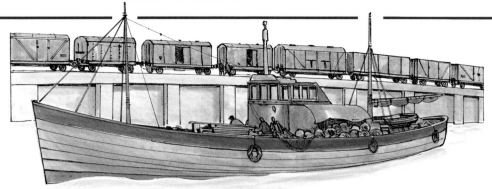

*These fishing boats were used to catch herring off the west coast of Scotland. Their catch was loaded into railroad cars.*

*These Brazilian fishermen are using poles with nets to catch mullet, a fish that lives in warm waters.*

*Crabs and lobsters are caught in sunken baskets baited with meat. They crawl inside to eat the meat and become trapped.*

People enjoy eating fish. But catching fish is sometimes not much fun. It is hard, wet, smelly work, and it can be dangerous. The crews of fishing boats have to go where fish can be found. In northern seas, boats risk sinking if they become coated with ice. In southern oceans boats face enormous waves and attacks from sharks.

Big fish are caught with hooks and lines, or driven into a netting cage between boats, then speared. Smaller fish are scooped up in nets.

# FISHING BOATS

**Modern** deep-sea trawlers catch fish, such as cod and haddock, for food. Radar detectors help them find large schools of fish.

**Factory ships** spend weeks at sea. The fish they catch are cleaned and gutted, then frozen to keep them fresh.

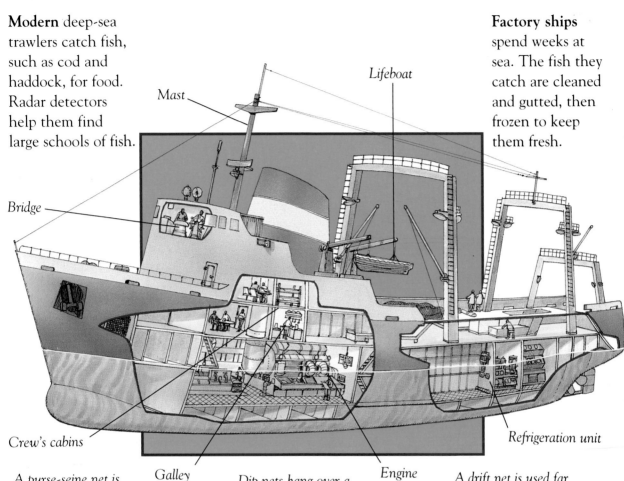

Mast

Lifeboat

Bridge

Crew's cabins

Galley (kitchen)

Engine room

Refrigeration unit

A purse-seine net is used to catch fish that live near the sea's surface. Once the fish are inside, they cannot escape.

Dip nets hang over a ship's side. They are very heavy when they are full of fish. Machines are needed to haul them on board.

A drift net is used far out at sea to catch fish that live in deep waters. They drift with the tides under the water and catch many fish.

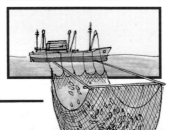

Travel by ship is slow, but it is cheap – especially if you are transporting large cargoes around the world. In the past, goods used to be packed into baskets, boxes, and bales of different shapes and sizes. Dockers loaded them by hand on to the ships.

Today, most cargo travels in sealed containers, and is loaded and unloaded by machine. Some ships have flat decks to carry timber. Others are refrigerated, to carry frozen food. Huge supertankers transport oil and gas.

**Container ships** carry metal containers filled with cargo. These can be loaded by cranes straight onto a truck or railroad wagon at the dock. The goods inside do not need to be unpacked.

# CARGO SHIPS

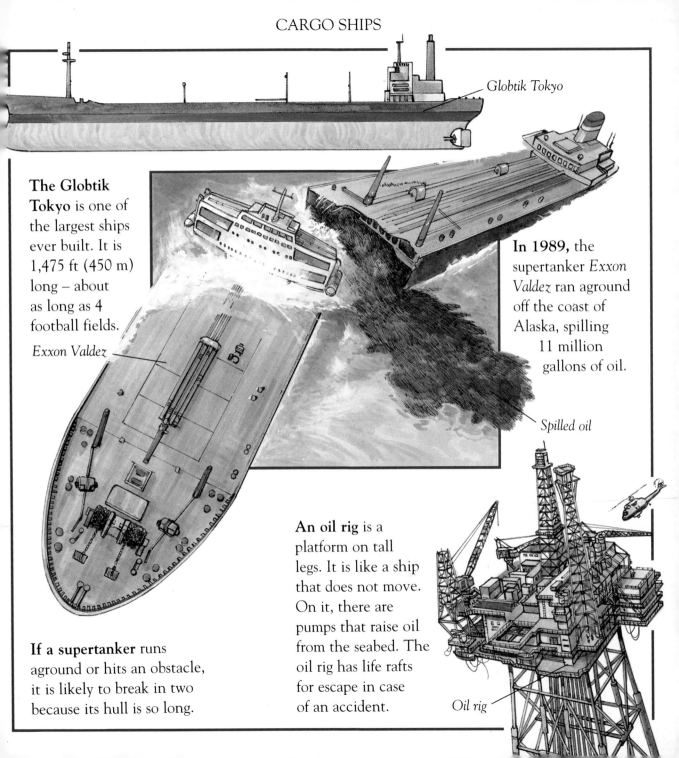

*Globtik Tokyo*

**The Globtik Tokyo** is one of the largest ships ever built. It is 1,475 ft (450 m) long – about as long as 4 football fields.

*Exxon Valdez*

**In 1989,** the supertanker *Exxon Valdez* ran aground off the coast of Alaska, spilling 11 million gallons of oil.

*Spilled oil*

**If a supertanker** runs aground or hits an obstacle, it is likely to break in two because its hull is so long.

**An oil rig** is a platform on tall legs. It is like a ship that does not move. On it, there are pumps that raise oil from the seabed. The oil rig has life rafts for escape in case of an accident.

*Oil rig*

**Dinghies** are small sailboats. There is room for only one or two people aboard. They are easy to handle.

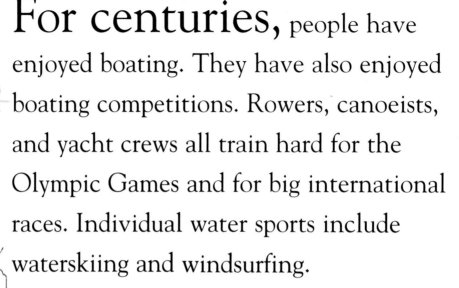

**Motorboats** have oil-powered engines. They are used to carry people on pleasure cruises.

# For centuries, people have enjoyed boating. They have also enjoyed boating competitions. Rowers, canoeists, and yacht crews all train hard for the Olympic Games and for big international races. Individual water sports include waterskiing and windsurfing.

In some parts of the world, people live in houseboats. This may be because there are no spare houses on land. Some houseboats are used for vacations.

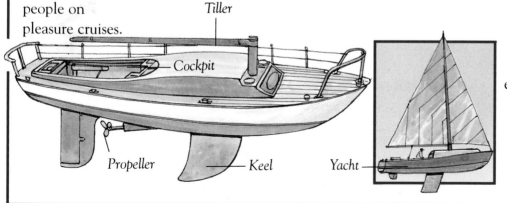

*Tiller*

*Cockpit*

*Propeller*

*Keel*

*Yacht*

**Big, luxurious yachts** are very expensive but there are many smaller, cheaper ones. Yacht clubs help members improve their sailing skills.

**Canals** are waterways made by people. In the 19th century, narrow boats were built as homes for traders who worked along the canals.

*Boats on the river in Bangkok, Thailand, are used as homes and as market stalls. Tourists enjoy visiting the floating markets.*

*Narrow boats are now used for holidays.*

*In Hong Kong, whole families live in cramped conditions on houseboats.*

**Beautiful house-boats** are moored in Kashmir, India. Some are used for tourists.

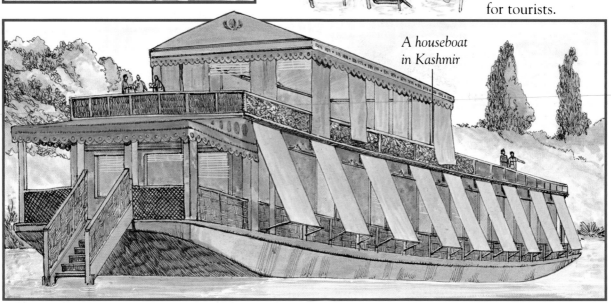

*A houseboat in Kashmir*

# USEFUL WORDS

**Bridge** Platform on deck, where a ship's captain stands to steer.

**Crew** People who operate the ship and look after the passengers.

**Cruise** Voyage, often just for pleasure.

**Flotation compartment** Section of a ship filled with air or foam to help keep it afloat.

**Hull** Part of ship that sits in water.

**Junk** Sailing ship from China and the Far East.

**Keel** Wooden beam that forms the backbone of a ship's hull.

**Man-of-war** Used to describe European warships from around 1600 to 1850.

**Mast** Strong wooden or metal pole used to support the ship's sails.

**Periscope** Tube with mirrors used by submarines to see above water.

**Propeller** Wooden or metal blades that spin around quickly, pushing a boat through the water.

**Rigging** Ropes used to support masts and sails.

**Radar** Way of finding out the position of other ships (and planes) using soundless radio waves.

**Rudder** Paddle at the back of a ship, and used to steer.

**SOS** Signal sent by code in an emergency.

**Scurvy** Disease caused by a lack of fresh fruit and vegetables.

**Tiller** Handle used to steer by moving a ship's rudder.

**Triere** Greek or Roman warship with three banks of oars.

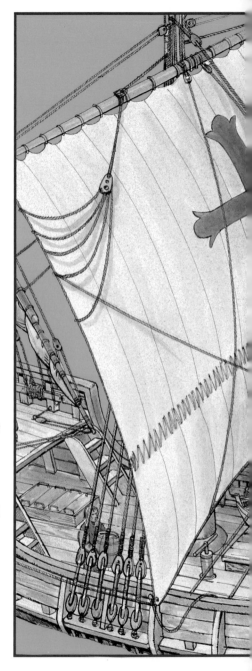

# INDEX